D0368934

Perfect Cocktails

Perfect Cocktails

The Essential Guide

Marthe Le Van

LARK BOOKS

A Division of Sterling Publishing Co., Inc.
New York

Art Director:
Tom Metcalf

Photography:
Evan Bracken

Photography Stylist:
Theresa Gwynn

Proofreader:
Kim Catanzarite

Library of Congress Cataloging -in- Publication Data

Le Van, Marthe
    Perfect cocktails: the essential guide / by Marthe Le Van.
        p. cm.
    Includes index
    ISBN 1-57990-245-6
    1. Cocktails. I. Title.

TX951.L42 2001
641.8'74–dc21

                                                    CIP
10 9 8 7 6 5 4 3 2   00-067818

Published by Lark Books, a division of
Sterling Publishing Co., Inc.
387 Park Avenue South, New York, N.Y. 10016

© 2001, Lark Books

Distributed in Canada by Sterling Publishing,
c/o Canadian Manda Group, One Atlantic Ave., Suite 105
Toronto, Ontario, Canada M6K 3E7

Distributed in the U.K. by Guild of Master Craftsman Publications
Ltd., Castle Place, 166 High Street, Lewes, East Sussex, England
BN7 1XU
Tel: (+ 44) 1273 477374, Fax: (+ 44) 1273 478606, Email:
pubs@thegmcgroup.com, Web: www.gmcpublications.com

Distributed in Australia by Capricorn Link (Australia) Pty Ltd.
P.O. Box 704, Windsor, NSW 2756, Australia

If you have questions or comments about this book, please contact:
Lark Books
67 Broadway
Asheville, NC 28801
(828) 236-9730

Printed in Hong Kong

Table of Contents

Introduction

Cocktail lounges are hot and Dean Martin's cool. A secret agent's Vodka Martini—shaken, not stirred—is all the rage. Think you're time traveling? Think again. Join a new breed of stylish hipsters around the world in celebrating the revival of classic cocktails. If you can measure, shake, and pour you're on your way to acquiring a wildly popular new hobby. Let this book be your guide as you teach yourself bartending and sample the delights of classic cocktails.

Cocktails should be for drinking, not stressing over. Starting a bar at home is instantly gratifying, and you don't have to spend a fortune to do it. Begin by selecting an appealing recipe and purchasing its ingredients. If you repeat this practice, gradually you'll be well stocked for any occasion. Understanding your ingredients is key. Shopping at the liquor store will be easier as you learn more about alcoholic beverages. Mixers and garnishes are quickly found at your local grocery. You may already have several of the more common items right in your refrigerator. Most of the tools for mixing, garnishing, and serving cocktails are already in your kitchen drawers and cabinets. It's simply a matter of how you look at things. An everyday tumbler can be a highball glass. A vegetable peeler can be a garnishing wonder wand.

Choosing a perfect cocktail, one that enhances the mood or menu of a special occasion, transforms an ordinary gathering into an unforgettable one. Many hosts go to great lengths preparing for a party, yet overlook the significance of distinctive drinks. Knowing what kind of cocktail will complement a specific event can be helpful to the host. Audition new recipes with your friends. As with any new skill, your talent and confidence will improve with practice. Making perfect cocktails will challenge your skills, feed your imagination, and delight and inspire others.

Excess is definitely out. Today's discerning palette values quality more than quantity. The recipes in this book encourage responsible drinking, which is vital to the modern, more health-conscious lifestyle. Classic cocktails aren't trendy concoctions with outrageous names developed more for potency than for taste. These time-honored libations succeed because of the harmonious flavors of their components. Once blended, they unite to form a more elaborate and tasteful drink. Learning to appreciate and linger over an exceptional drink will help you keep track of your alcoholic consumption.

Cocktails have a long and colorful history. Whether they conjure up scenes of movie stars at the Polo Lounge or high rollers by a Las Vegas pool, the romance of this cosmopolitan culture has great nostalgic appeal. In no time at all you'll be mixing perfect cocktails in the seasoned tradition of the model bartender, trustworthy and astute, but with a charm and dignity that is all your own. A toast—to the beginning of a beautiful friendship!

Glossary of Terms

To be conversant in the cocktail culture, your first hurdle is learning the language. Initially, many bartending terms and phrases can be confusing. Acquainting yourself with the vocabulary not only insures your success as a drink mixer, but also encourages placing and receiving accurate drink requests.

Aperitif. A refreshing drink served before dinner to stimulate the appetite. Typically includes gin, vermouth, or Campari. Many of the oldest cocktails are aperitifs. See page 102 for recommendations.

Blend. When one batch of liquor combines with another during the production of alcohol. Frequently refers to whiskey.

Build. To pour drink ingredients directly into the serving glass.

Call drink. To request a brand name liquor when ordering a drink. Typically more expensive than the house brand.

Chaser. A mixer served independently for sipping along with alcohol or after a shot. Also known as a side, or a back.

Cocktail. A drink that combines one or more alcoholic beverages. Can include flavoring agents. Often served chilled. Strictly short and neat.

Cordial. The infusion of fruits, herbs, spices, and other plants with liquor such as whiskey or brandy. Active flavoring agents for cocktails. Interchangeable with liqueur. See pages 16–19 for examples.

Dash. The smallest bar measurement specifying a quantity of liquid. Approximately $\frac{1}{32}$ oz (1.2 mL).

Digestif. A drink served after dinner to complete the meal. Also a nightcap. Often sweet. See page 103 for suggestions.

Double. A drink made with twice the amount of liquor called for in the standard version.

Dry. Suggests the quantity of dry vermouth in a cocktail. Less dry vermouth will result in a drier cocktail. Particularly relevant to the Martini.

Float. To carefully pour a small amount of liquid to balance as the top layer of a drink. Use the back of a spoon to gently disperse the ingredient.

Liqueur. See cordial.

Liquor. A beverage distilled from alcohol. Any organic substance that ferments can be a principle ingredient. Routinely gleaned from grains and fruits. Acts as the foundation of most cocktails and mixed drinks. The six primary types are brandy, gin, rum, tequila, vodka, and whiskey. Also called spirits. See pages 13–15 for descriptions.

Mixed drink. A drink that combines one or more alcoholic beverages with flavoring agents. Strictly tall and on the rocks.

Mixer. Any nonalcoholic beverage employed as an ingredient of a mixed drink. Often waters, juices, or sodas.

Neat. A drink that is served with no ice or mixer.

On the rocks. A drink served over ice cubes.

Perfect. A drink made with equal parts of sweet and dry vermouth when vermouth appears as an ingredient.

Plain. See neat.

Proof. The American standard for alcohol content.
Proof ÷ 2 = percentage of alcohol.

Shake. To mix and chill the ingredients of a cocktail by
shaking a sealed container.

Short. A small drink served in a 2–3 oz (60–90 mL) glass.

Splash. A small bar measurement that specifies a quantity of liquid
just under $\frac{1}{2}$ oz (15 mL). Often just a quick squirt over a drink.
Larger than a dash.

Stir. A way to mix and chill a drink using a bar spoon.
Stir drinks in a serving glass, mixing glass, or pitcher.

Straight up. See neat.

Tall. A large drink served in a glass that holds 5 oz
(150 mL) or more. Also a drink served in a larger glass to
hold more mixer.

Virgin. A cocktail made without its alcoholic ingredients.

Indispensable Liquors

*L*earning about liquors can be a lifelong passion. Few people venture into this fascinating world, content to champion one favorite beverage. The "white" liquors, such as gin, rum, and vodka, appear to be more widely palatable. Their popularity, however, may not stem from taste so much as mixability. Appraising the "brown" liquors is where true reverence is born. Brandy, whiskey, and tequila exhibit deep and complex flavors. Analyzing their intensity will enable you to grow more enlightened with every encounter.

Brandy

*B*randy is the classification for liquor made from fermented grape wine. This category also includes all spirits distilled from other fruits, such as apples, pears, cherries, plums, apricots, and berries. Although brandy comes from fruit, fruit-flavored brandies are cordials.

There are four steps in the production of brandy. The first is fermenting the fruit. The second and third are distilling the alcohol into brandy and aging it in oak casks. Once the aging is complete, the final step is to blend the liquor to taste. Familiar varieties of brandy include Cognac, Armagnac, calvados, ouzo, and kirsch.

Gin

*G*in is a grain distillate with added flavorings. Gin receives its distinctive taste largely from juniper berries. Other contributing spices include bitter almonds, cardamom, caraway, citrus peel, and licorice.

There is no aging process in gin production. Once distillation and seasoning are complete, gin is ready to drink. Because the quality of gin varies widely, it's advisable to stick to the premium brands.

Rum

At the heart of rum production is sugar cane. Distillers turn its sweet juices into molasses, and then ferment the syrup into rum. Straight rum is available in three distinct varieties depending upon the cask used in the aging process. Light rum ages in stainless steel tanks. Gold or amber rum matures in an oak cask. Dark rum results from a charred oak barrel. Flavored rums, known as spiced, are also produced. Cachaça is a Brazilian liquor that differs from rum by bypassing the molasses state. Distillers manufacture cachaça directly from sugar cane juice.

Tequila

The source of tequila is the heart of the blue agave plant. Before distillation, workers trim, grate, cook to a paste, and then compress the plant for its juices. The varying colors of tequila signify different degrees of aging. Tequila turns darker the longer it remains in the barrel.

By law, tequila can only come from the Jalisco region of Mexico. Mezcal is any liquor comparable to tequila, but distilled in a different location. Legends about powerful worms in tequila bottles have no merit. Their presence is simply a marketing strategy.

Vodka

Though fermenting and distilling grain is the standard method of making vodka, it can also originate from other food plants. Beets and potatoes are two such alternatives. Like gin, vodka requires no aging and is ready for drinking immediately after distillation. Perhaps the most mixable liquor, vodka has no distinct taste, color, or aroma. Current trends reflect a taste for vodka infused with fruit or spice flavorings. Lemon, berry, and pepper vodkas are among the most popular.

Whiskey

All whiskeys have a grain base and undergo oak-cask aging. Beyond this, whiskey expands into a vibrant spectrum of categories and tastes. Even spelling is an issue. Whiskey is spelled with an "e" if it's of Irish or American origin. The Scotch and the Canadians drop the "e" from the word. These four nationalities also provide the four principal varieties of whiskey.

The strong flavor of Irish whiskey comes from its rich casks. They once held robust sherry, rum, or bourbon. The Irish use coal to dry the barley malt used in their whiskeys whereas Scotch whiskey, better known as Scotch, is dried over peat. Peat-fire drying imparts an intense, smoky flavor to the whiskey. As with other whiskey, Scotch becomes smoother the longer it ages in the cask. No whiskey matures after bottling.

Of the American whiskeys, bourbon is the most dominant. By law, bourbon must contain at least 51 percent corn. Barley and rye comprise the remaining base grains. Bourbon's trace of sweetness and vanilla finish comes from its charred oak cask. In Tennessee whiskey, charcoal filtration produces a balanced taste. The final American whiskey types are rye and corn. These are not as prevalent as bourbon and Tennessee whiskey. Canadian whiskey is often light and gentle. Its pleasing character comes from attentive blending. Rye is the chief component of Canadian whiskey.

Liqueurs and Fortified Wines

$\mathcal{A}$lthough the foundation of every liqueur is a basic spirit, the diversity of flavors created through redistillation appears endless. Every imaginable fusion of fruit, nut, and spice competes to tempt your taste buds.

You may want to evaluate the characteristics of a straight liqueur before combining it into a cocktail. Many liqueurs make excellent drinks on their own. Begin by reading the bottle for interesting information on the liqueur's origins, ingredients, and distillation techniques. Pour a taste and notice the pigment of the liqueur and its thickness. You can use these observations later to design layered drinks. Sniff the aroma of the liqueur. Does it have one dominant scent or a complex bouquet? If the scent is complex, can you pick out certain components? Lastly, take a sip. Do you taste what your nose suspected? How does the liqueur feel on your tongue? Is there any distinct aftertaste? Following these taste test guidelines for all alcoholic beverages will yield a wise palette.

Apricot, **cherry**, and **peach brandy** are all brandy wines fortified with fruit nectar.

Bénédictine receives its slightly sweet essence from the infusion of nearly 30 herbs and spices into Cognac. Of note, Bénédictine contains cardamom, nutmeg, cloves, myrrh, and vanilla. The original recipe was given to Bénédictine monks in the 16th century. It's a choice after-dinner drink.

Campari is a liqueur established in Italy in 1860. Produced from herbs and citrus fruits, Campari is an integral ingredient in aperitifs. Campari's bright red color trumpets its presence in any drink.

Chartreuse's strong flavor is the result of blending more than 130 herbs and spices with wine. Yellow Chartreuse is milder than the green variety. The secret recipe for this liqueur was given to Carthusian monks in 17th-century France.

Cointreau, the prevailing brand of triple sec, consists of sweet and bitter orange peels flavoring high-quality brandy.

Crème de is a French phrase. It implies a liqueur with a thick viscosity. The word that follows *de* suggests its flavoring.

Crème de cacao gets its chocolate flavor from cacao beans and vanilla. White crème de cacao is, in truth, clear. It's milder than the dark (brown) variety.

Crème de cassis comes from French black currants, fruits, and berries.

Crème de menthe is a combination of mint and spearmint. Both green and white crème de menthe taste the same.

Curaçao is a type of triple sec made from the peel of a bittersweet orange grown in the Dutch West Indies. Its three color varieties, clear, orange, and blue, have an identical taste.

Drambuie is a mix of Scotch whiskey, heather honey, herbs, and spices.

Dubonnet is wine fortified with grape brandy. It's a popular, bittersweet aperitif flavored with several dozen natural ingredients including herbs, flowers, spices, roots, peels, and seeds. Dubonnet is available in white and red.

Galliano Liquore's primary flavoring is anise seed accompanied by vanilla, lavender, yarrow musk, juniper, and more than 30 other ingredients. An Italian product, Galliano's eccentric long bottles are easy to recognize.

Kahlúa tastes like coffee but expands with additional aromas of vanilla, chocolate, and coconut.

Maraschino's character comes from a sour cherry, called the marasca, aided by pure cane syrup. It's processed and distilled like brandy.

Pernod is a frequent substitute for absinthe. It's a secret blend of plant extracts mixed with distilled alcohol and water.

Sherry is a fortified wine made from white grapes produced exclusively in the Andalusian region of Spain. There are two major types of sherry. Finos are pale, light wines, while olorosos are dark, heavy wines. Sherry's wide range of colors and flavors is the result of different distillation processes and sugar content. Sherries don't carry a vintage date, as they are blended over many years from cask to cask. This maintains a consistency of flavor. Very dry sherry makes a tasteful aperitif.

Triple sec gets its name from a distillation process. Sec means dry. Triple sec means triple dried, or triple distilled. It's a useful orange-flavored liqueur.

Vermouth is wine infused with herbs, alcohol, sugar, caramel, and water. Although most people enjoy drinking fortified wines—such as Madeira, port, and sherry—straight, vermouth is highly mixable and a key ingredient in many drinks. Vermouth comes in four general varieties, although recipes differ from brand to brand. Dry and extra-dry vermouth is white, or bianco. Sweet vermouth is usually red, or rosso, but is also available in white. The last category, rosé, is semisweet. Vermouth is perishable and will spoil if stored unopened for too long. Unlike most liqueurs, vermouth requires refrigeration. As with bitters, use vermouth judiciously. Calibrate your pour to the taste of each individual.

Wine and Champagne factor in a few delicious cocktails. You don't have to purchase top brands when these ingredients merge with others. Reserve fine wines and Champagnes for drinking on their own.

Mixers

Mixers are nonalcoholic liquids used to flavor and/or dilute an alcoholic beverage. A wide selection of mixers is a worthwhile addition to any bar. The number of mixers you stock directly influences the diversity of drinks you can offer. Left unopened, most mixers have a long shelf-life. If you find durable staples, such as tonic water, club soda, or ginger ale at a discount price, it's beneficial to purchase a substantial supply.

Juices

$\int$ emon and lime juices are the two chief mixers of any bar. Orange, cranberry, and grapefruit juice make up the second tier of bar juices. Coconut, pineapple, and tomato juice, though rarely needed, are welcome additions. Always remember that fresh-squeezed juices taste best and make the finest drinks. If you're mixing a pitcher of cocktails, use an electric juicer rather than a manual press to squeeze the fresh ingredients. This will reduce time and labor. Rose's Lime Juice, a bottled brand, is a respectable substitute for fresh-squeezed.

Waters

$\int$ o cover the basics, such as Scotch & Soda or Gin & Tonic, several waters qualify as required mixers. Club soda and tonic water provide the taste and gusto of old-fashioned seltzer. Mineral water and sparkling water are not only thirst-quenching but, with a twist, make great "mocktails" for nondrinkers.

Sodas

$\int$ ike water, soda is often a primary mixer. A supply of cola, lemon-lime soda, and ginger ale will service most requests.

Dairy

$\mathcal{M}$ any drinks, such as the Alexander and Grasshopper, call for heavy (or whipping) cream. The diet-conscious can substitute light cream, half and half, or milk, to cut down on fat. Remember to keep dairy products refrigerated to maintain freshness, and check expiration dates carefully. If the product is questionable, test it before serving to your guests.

Sour mix

Sour mix, or sweet and sour mix, has effectively replaced the traditional method of combining sugar and lemon juice. Using a sour mix speeds the process of bartending, but many people feel the integrity of the drink is sacrificed by the omission of fresh juice. The recipes in this book don't use sour mix; however, any sour, collins, or fizz recipe is easily adapted.

Seasonings

From sweet to hot to tart, seasonings play a prominent role in the total cocktail experience. They contribute many intense flavors that don't exist in beverage form.

Bitters

Several types of bitters, pivotal to many recipes, are available. Angostura bitters, made from rare, tropical herbs and spices, is the most widely recognized brand. Developed in Venezuela for medicinal purposes, the original Angostura recipe has been a closely held secret since 1824. Peychaud bitters are common in New Orleans, Louisiana. Its recipe was imported from Haiti. The popularity of the Sazerac cocktail, see page 91, helped to create a demand for Peychaud bitters. Most other bitters are derived from fruits, such as the orange or peach. Use bitters sparingly—their flavor is strong.

Sweeteners

*F*our forms of dry sugar are very useful to have at the bar. These are granulated sugar, powdered sugar, brown sugar, and sugar cubes. In hot drinks, honey can serve as an alternative sweetener. Two other sweeteners, grenadine and sugar syrup, merit a closer look.

Grenadine

*G*renadine is the most popular fruit syrup in cocktail recipes. It's a strong sweetener made from pomegranate juice. Grenadine's unique color brings a rosy pink hue to many drinks.

Sugar syrup

*U*sing a sugar syrup eliminates the difficulty of dissolving dry sugar in cool liquids. Sugar syrup can be made in advance if stored in a cool place. To make sugar syrup, you'll need 1 pound (.46 kg) of granulated sugar, and 1 1/2 cups (.36 L) of hot water. Place both ingredients in a small sauce pan. Slowly bring the liquid to a boil. Skim the top of the mixture and cool completely. Pour the syrup into a container and store.

Other syrups

*O*rgeat is an almond-flavored syrup made from sugar, orange flower water, and almonds. It's thick, sweet, and cloudy. Passion fruit syrup, also known as maracuja syrup, is made from a small tropical fruit. The best quality available uses pure cane sugar.

Spices

Sweet spices, such as fresh ground nutmeg, cloves, and cinnamon sticks flatter hot toddies and many dairy drinks. Pungent seasonings, such as black pepper, celery salt, horseradish, Worcestershire, and hot pepper sauce yield a consummate Bloody Mary. A supply of table or rock salt should be available for rimming glasses or shooting tequila. Plant extracts, such as rose oil and orange blossom water can bring exotic nuances to classic cocktails.

Garnishes

Garnishes are the edible trimmings that adorn many cocktails. A great drink garnish provides both decorative flair and elevated flavor. Certain drinks have traditional garnishes while others are ripe for artistic embellishment. There are a few important strategies to keep in mind while musing on your next creation. First, make sure the garnish is edible and that its taste suits that of the drink. Also, the size and complexity of the garnish should never be an obstruction. When a garnish is listed as an ingredient, always reserve it for the final decoration of the serving glass. Never add the garnish to the shaker or mixing glass with the other ingredients.

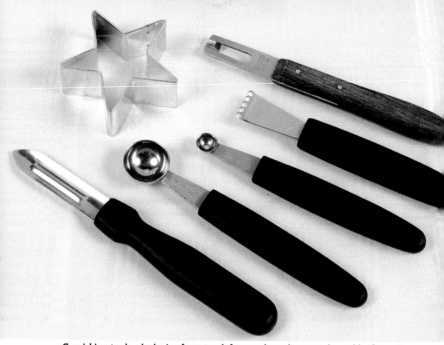

Garnishing tools, clockwise from top left: star-shaped cutter, channel knife, zester, small melon baller, large melon baller, vegetable peeler

Garnishing tools

*Y*ou need only a few basic tools to skillfully garnish. Use a large kitchen knife to make the initial cuts in fruits. Paring knives have small, sharp blades and are ideal for executing precise cuts with ease. A more unusual gadget is the channel knife, or zester. Its v-shaped blade shears fruit rind for twists or zests. A vegetable peeler with a sharp blade is a sound, economical substitute for a channel knife. The final utensil is the melon baller, which looks like a tiny ice cream scoop. Most melon ballers come with two scoops of different sizes, one on either end.

Fruit

 resh seasonal fruit will produce the most attractive and appetizing garnishes. Look for unblemished and even-colored peels on lemons and limes. Thin skins on these fruits often indicate more juice. Melons that have just begun to ripen have firm flesh and conform well to the shape of the garnish. Wash all fresh fruits before use and remove any seeds. Fruit garnishes can be cut in advance but will dry out over time. To retain moisture, either cover precut fruits with a damp paper towel and refrigerate until use, or spritz them with a little club soda.

Assorted garnishes

Twists

 twist is a narrow strip of lemon peel. When making a twist, attempt to remove only the yellow part of the peel, as the white layer underneath, the pith, tastes bitter. The easiest way to cut a twist is to use a channel knife or sharp vegetable peeler. With practice, successful twists can be cut with a paring knife. Twists should be approximately ¼ inch (.63 cm) wide and 1 to 1 ½ inches (2.5 to 3.75 cm) long. The purpose of a twist is to disburse aromatic lemon oil into a drink. To accomplish this, grasp both ends of the peel and bend them in opposite directions. Drop the bent twist into the drink.

Garnishes on a cutting board with a large kitchen knife and a small paring knife

Twist variations

A long spiral of citrus peel is a bold and festive garnish. Begin peeling a strip at one end of your lemon, lime, or orange. Spiral your way down and around the fruit's circumference, trimming away one continuous strip until you reach your desired length. To create an elegant knotted twist, start with a section of peel that is ¼ inch (.63 cm) wide and 3 to 4 inches (7.5 to 10 cm) long. Tie a single knot in the middle to release the citrus essence, and drop the twist into the drink.

Wedges

*W*hen someone requests a squeeze for their beverage, a wedge is the proper garnish. The fruit juice squeezed from a wedge becomes an active cocktail ingredient. To form a wedge, first cut either a lemon, lime, or orange in half lengthwise. Then cut four or five wedges from each half. Finally, trim the angled sides of each wedge for easy squeezing, and make a straight cut to remove the pith from the center. This extra step reduces the chance of juice squirting into your eyes.

Slices

*G*arnishing with a slice of fruit mainly serves a decorative purpose. Though slices are not for squeezing, they can be eaten. To create slices, cut the fruit in half horizontally (not through the stem and navel end). Make subsequent horizontal slices approximately ⅜ inch (.95 cm) thick and remove all seeds. At this stage, slices may be cut in half or left whole. If you're using a whole slice, you may want to cut a notch from the skin to the center of the fruit and slip it over the lip of the glass. Style lemons, limes, or oranges in this manner.

Melon balls

*T*he subtle shades and flavors of melon balls are tasteful alternatives to citrus garnishes. Honeydew, cantaloupe, and watermelon are outstanding for brunch drinks. Try using different-size scoops to form melon balls, then arrange them imaginatively on a skewer.

Celery stalk

A celery stalk is the traditional Bloody Mary garnish. It's important to wash celery thoroughly to remove dirt. Peel away those pesky threads with a vegetable peeler or paring knife, then cut the stalk to fit your serving glass. The leafy tops of the stalk can give extra character to your presentation.

Out of the jar

*M*any traditional garnishes require no preparation and very little maintenance. The most work you will do is to spear them on a skewer. They should, however, always be on hand. Garnishes of this type include olives, maraschino cherries, and cocktail onions. There is a wide variety of olives to choose from. Try several types to see which ones match your taste. Maraschino cherries and cocktail onions are standard fare. Buy stemmed maraschino cherries; they will be easier for you and your guests to manage.

One unusual classic

*I*f you are serving a Pimm's Cup, have cucumbers handy. Custom dictates the appropriate garnish for Pimm's is the dark green skin of the cucumber. The flesh can be left on, as in a slice, or you can make a twist from just the peel.

Trimming the rim

*S*how your style by applying a ribbon of salt or sugar around the rim of a cocktail glass. This technique is a definite crowd pleaser. Spread a thin layer, approximately ¼ inch (6 mm) deep, of salt or sugar over a saucer or small plate. Use a lemon or orange wedge, or, to be truly elegant, a trace of liqueur, to moisten the rim of the glass. The rim should be damp about ¼ inch (6 mm) down from the top of the glass on both the interior and exterior sides. Turn the glass over and dip it into the sugar or salt. Pour your cocktail and enjoy!

Know Your Tools

𝒴our home bar will operate smoothly with all the right tools. Fortunately, most of these supplies are common kitchen utensils and can be unearthed without too much trouble. The tools in the first list will receive heavy use and should be assembled without delay. As your skill builds, it may be fun to gather the tools on the second list. These may encourage further experimentation.

Bartending tools on a cutting board, clockwise from top left: Boston shaker, three-part shaker, double-headed jigger, bar spoon, paring knife, waiter's friend, strainer

Essential Utensils

Bar spoon. Use this efficient tool to stir drinks, measure small amounts, muddle ingredients, layer cordials, and grab garnishes. Your bar spoon should have a handle at least 10 inches (25.4 cm) long. Most bar spoons are made of metal.

Bar towel. Any absorbent towel or rag will do to clean up spills and condensation.

Can and bottle opener. Indispensable for fruit juice and beer bottles, some openers also include a corkscrew and knife. These combination tools are called a waiter's friend. The knife is handy for splitting seals on wine bottles.

Cocktail shaker. Use one of these to simultaneously mix and chill drinks. The cocktail shaker comes in three main designs. The three-part shaker consists of a metal tumbler, a snugly-fitting lid, and a small cap that fits over the lid. The cap covers a built-in strainer. The two-part shaker has a mixing tumbler and a lid. No cap is required, as the two-part shaker doesn't have a built-in strainer. The Boston shaker is the most modern style. It's used by professional bartenders for its speed. The Boston shaker is composed of a 16-oz (490 mL) metal tumbler, preferably stainless steel, and a 12-oz (360 mL) thick-walled, straight-sided, glass tumbler. The metal tumbler over-laps the glass. Unlike the classic shakers, Boston shakers are a two-handed operation (see pages 35–37 for shaking instructions).

Corkscrew. Given the profusion of designs, the most important considerations in acquiring a corkscrew are comfort and ease. The worm style, with its open, spiralling point, is a sensible choice. Worm corkscrews are often combined with a bottle and can opener on a device known as a waiter's friend.

Cutting board. A bartender's cutting board should be moderately sized. Wood, plastic, marble, or glass are the choice surfaces for slicing fruit garnishes.

Ice bucket. Having a fresh supply of ice cubes within arm's reach will make your bar run smoothly. An ice bucket should hold a minimum of three trays of ice cubes. It's a good idea to make or purchase extra cubes for gatherings.

Ice tongs or **ice scoop.** Use either of these to dispense ice cubes from the ice bucket. Avoid using your hands.

Jigger. This measuring cup regulates the amount of alcohol to be mixed into a drink. Jiggers come in many sizes because standard pours differ from bar to bar. Most jiggers are double-headed, meaning they have measuring cups on either end. These cups differ in capacity by approximately $\frac{1}{2}$ oz (15 mL). The larger cup is generally 1 to 2 oz (30 to 60 mL) while the smaller cup, or pony, is $\frac{1}{2}$ to $1\frac{1}{2}$ oz (15-45 mL). Purchase a sturdy jigger with a prominent lip to lessen messy drips and spills.

Mixing glass. This oversized tumbler is used for stirring individual drinks that are not created directly in their serving glass. It's convenient to use the glass section of a Boston shaker as your mixing glass. Always rinse your mixing glass between drinks.

Paring knife. This is a small kitchen knife with a sharp blade for cutting garnishes.

Pitcher. An excellent container for mixing multiple stirred drinks, pitchers also provide more graceful service of juices and water.

Strainer. Blocking ice from pouring into a drink is an important task. This flat, spoon-shaped utensil has a flexible spring attached around its lip that fits over a shaker or mixing glass. Rows of holes allow the liquid to freely flow into the glass.

Trash receptacles. Dispose of paper and food waste properly to keep your bar clean and appealing.

Advanced Supplies

Bottle or speed pourers. These plastic or metal devices fit over the mouth of liquor bottles. They have a permanent spout that regulates the flow of liquid. With practice, speed pourers allow you to mix drinks without the use of a jigger.

Bottle stoppers. Replace cumbersome screw tops or corks with easy and durable bottle stoppers.

Dash bottles. Similar in form and function to a cruet, this vessel strictly regulates the flow of flavoring ingredients. Dash bottles are particularly effective for dispensing bitters or vermouth, as they distribute their contents one drop at a time.

Electric blender. When crushing ice, an electric blender should have a powerful engine and sharp blades. A blender is required to make frozen drinks.

Fruit juicer. Fresh-squeezed juice is the mark of a superior drink. A manual juicer should fulfill your needs.

Grater. The manual kitchen variety pulverizes spices, such as nutmeg, for garnishing.

Muddler. Grind fruit or herbs into a paste with this wooden pestle. Its bat-shaped handle should be long enough to reach the bottom of any serving glass. Muddlers also help dissolve sugars and release essential oils.

Measuring spoons. Use these tools when recipes call for small quantities.

Recycling bins. Sorting bottles and cans as you tend bar will make for a speedy clean up and set a good example for your guests.

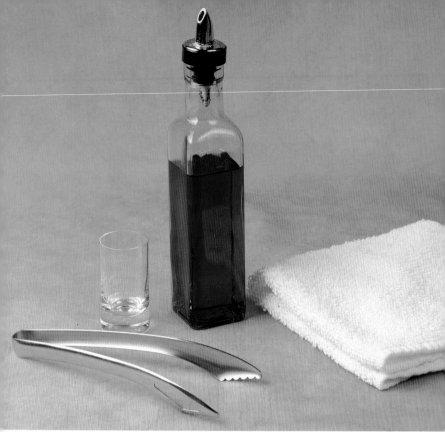

Bartending tools, clockwise from top left: shot glass, dash bottle, bar towel, ice tongs

Presentation Supplies

Coasters. Place these under glasses to control the spread of condensation, thereby limiting water damage to furniture. Coasters also muffle the sound of glasses hitting tables.

Cocktail napkins. Like coasters, these soak up condensation, reduce noise, and add a decorative element. Cocktail napkins also yield a better grip on drinking glasses.

Cocktail picks. These drink ornaments can range from simple skewers to outlandish umbrellas. Their sole function, however, is to support garnishes.

Straws. Available in a variety of lengths, disposable plastic straws function as sipping and stirring devices.

Swizzle sticks. Practical and attractive, these rods let guests continue stirring as they enjoy their cocktail.

Shake It Up

Shaken cocktails emerge cool, crisp, and concentrated. You'll grasp this simple technique in no time with these helpful hints. If your recipe calls for ice cubes, always place them in the shaker first. This will chill the shaker and cool the ingredients as they are added. Five or six cubes will be sufficient for one drink. Use less ice for two drinks so there's more room in the shaker. Don't overfill the shaker; the ingredients will need plenty of room to travel. Vigorously shake drinks that have many ingredients, or ingredients that don't easily mix. Cocktails that are blended and served frozen, such as Daiquiris and Piña Coladas, can be made by shaking their ingredients with crushed ice.

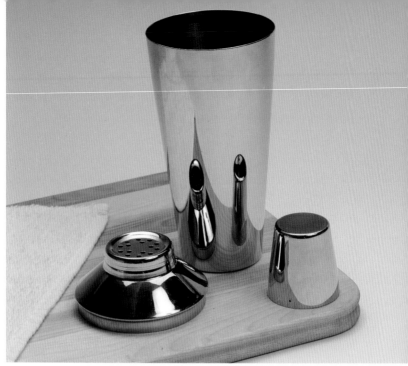

Three-part shaker

Using a traditional shaker

*P*our the ingredients for the selected drink into the metal container with ice cubes. Secure the lid on top of the container and form a tight seal. If there is a cap, place it on top of the lid to cover the strainer. Move the shaker in an up and down motion. Shake your drink for 10 to 20 seconds. Thin liquids that mix well will require a shorter shake than thicker ingredients. Place the shaker down when it feels very cold. Remove the lid or cap and strain the contents of the container into a glass.

Using a Boston shaker

*P*our the ingredients for the selected drink into the metal tumbler with ice cubes. Secure the mixing glass on top of the tumbler and form a tight seal. Using both hands, move the shaker in an up and down motion. The mixture should travel back and forth between the mixing glass and shaker. Shake your drink for 10 to 20 seconds. Thin liquids that mix well will require a shorter shake than thicker ingredients. When it feels very cold, place the shaker down, with the mixing glass on top. Break the seal between the mixing glass and the metal tumbler by hitting the tumbler with the heel of your hand. Remove the mixing glass, and strain the contents of the container into a glass.

Boston shaker

Glossary of Glass Design

*I*n theory it's simple: a bar glass should be compatible with the drink it holds. However, fastidious connoisseurs continue to promote the use of specialized glasses. This could make choosing glasses quite an ordeal. Fortunately, getting the ultimate set of bar glasses is an unnecessary goal. You need not be troubled if economic or storage limitations hamper your collection. It's better to keep your selection small, allowing a few glasses to perform multiple functions. At the very least you should have old-fashioned glasses, highball glasses, and red wine glasses. With these you'll be able to respectfully hold any mixed drink.

Champagne flute. A tall, tapered, 10 oz (300 mL) goblet uniquely designed for Champagne and Champagne cocktails.

Cocktail glass. A 3–6 oz (90–180 mL) goblet with a wide, angled bowl. Ideal for chilled neat drinks and frappes. Also known as a Martini glass.

Collins glass. A narrow, 8–12 oz (240–360 mL) tumbler. Also available in a tapered variety. Excellent for any collins drink. Can replace the highball glass.

Cordial glass. A miniature 1–1 ½ oz (30–45 mL) goblet. Ideal for sipping cordials and neat after-dinner drinks.

Highball glass. A large, 8–12 oz (240–360 mL) tumbler. Suitable for tall drinks, highballs, beers, and sodas.

Glassware, clockwise from top left: collins glass, Champagne flute, cocktail glass, Irish coffee glass, old-fashioned glass, shot glass, snifter

Irish coffee glass. An 8–12 oz (240–360 mL) heat-resistant, footed glass mug. Suitable for all hot mixed drinks.

Margarita glass. A stemmed goblet that holds 8–14 oz (240–420 mL). Has a wider and deeper bowl than the cocktail glass. Appropriate for all frozen mixed drinks.

Old-fashioned glass. A medium, 5–10 oz (150–300 mL) tumbler. Accommodates anything ordered on the rocks, and short mixed drinks with ice.

Pint glass. A tall, 14–16 oz (420–480 mL) tumbler. Fitting for beer and sodas.

Red wine goblet. Holds 5–10 oz (150–300 mL). Has a wider bowl and larger lip than a white wine goblet. An alternative to the cocktail glass.

Shot glass. A miniature tumbler that holds ¾–2 oz (22.5–60 mL). Used to serve straight shots of liquor, and as a measuring device.

Sour glass. A 4–8 oz (120–240 mL) goblet with a tall, narrow bowl. Appropriate for neat sours and cordials.

Snifter. A short-stemmed, 4–24 oz (120–720 mL) goblet with a broad-based bowl and mild taper. Designed for sipping unchilled neat liquors and liqueurs.

White wine goblet. Holds 5–10 oz (150–300 mL). Can service wine, cordials, port, or sherry.

Chilling Glasses

*Y*our cocktails will remain cold and fresh if served in a chilled glass. Use any of the following three methods to prepare your glasses for an iceless but cold drink. Time and space permitting, your first option is to place your cocktail glasses in the refrigerator or freezer for a few hours. Secondly, try plunging the bowls of the glasses into crushed ice for a few minutes. The third and fastest cooling method is to swirl ice cubes in the glass for one full minute.

Frosted glasses are a fantastic touch for frozen cocktails. Achieve a frosted glass by dipping the glass into water, shaking off the excess moisture, and then placing it into the freezer for several hours. Keep a few frosted glasses on hand for speedy chilling.

Know Your Basic Blends

*F*undamental ingredients or preparation methods classify some mixed drinks into distinguishing families with well-known names. Typically, these families give bartenders their principle instructions, and the consumer needs only to designate the desired liquor. Learning these basic blends will increase your mixing repertoire.

Basic Collins

1 1/2 oz (45 mL) desired liquor
1 oz (30 mL) lemon juice
1/2 oz (15 mL) sugar syrup
2 oz (60 mL) club soda
maraschino cherry for garnish
lemon slice for garnish

Pour the first three ingredients into a collins glass. Stir well. Fill the glass with ice cubes. Add the club soda. Garnish with the cherry and the lemon slice.

Basic Eggnog

5 oz (150 mL) milk
2 oz (60 mL) desired liquor
1 tsp (5 mL) sugar
1 egg yolk
ground nutmeg or cinnamon for garnish

Pour the ingredients into a shaker with ice cubes. Shake vigorously. Strain into a chilled old-fashioned glass. Garnish with a dusting of ground nutmeg or cinnamon.

Basic Fizz

4 oz (120 mL) club soda
2 oz (60 mL) desired liquor
1 oz (30 mL) lemon juice
1 tsp (5 mL) sugar

Pour the ingredients, including the club soda, into a shaker over ice cubes. Shake well. Pour into a collins glass. Foam will gather at the top.

Basic Flip

2 oz (60 mL) desired liquor
¾ oz (22.5 mL) cream
½ oz (15 mL) sugar syrup
1 egg yolk

Pour the ingredients into a shaker with ice cubes. Shake vigorously. Strain into a chilled cocktail glass.

Basic Frappé

2 oz (60 mL) desired liqueur

Fill a cocktail glass with shaved or crushed ice. Pour in the liqueur.

Basic Highball

2 oz (60 mL) desired liquor
water or club soda

Pour the liquor into a highball glass with ice cubes. Fill with water or club soda.

Basic Julep

4 oz (120 mL) desired liquor
2 sugar cubes
6–8 mint leaves
mint sprigs for garnish

Place the ingredients into a cocktail shaker. Muddle well to dissolve the sugar and release the oil and aroma from the mint leaves. Add ice cubes to the shaker. Shake well. Strain into a collins glass with ice cubes. Garnish with the mint sprigs.

Basic Pousse-Café

A minimum of 3 liquors and/or liqueurs of varying densities and colors

Pour each ingredient slowly over the back of a bar spoon into a cordial or shot glass. Begin with the heaviest liquor and proceed to the lightest. The layers should balance without blending.

Basic Rickie

lime wedge
5 oz (150 mL) club soda
2 oz (60 mL) desired liquor

Squeeze the lime juice from the wedge into a highball glass with ice cubes. Drop the wedge into the glass. Pour the remaining ingredients into the glass. Stir well.

Basic Sour

1½ oz (45 mL) desired liquor
1½ oz (45 mL) lemon juice
¾ oz (22.5 mL) sugar syrup
maraschino cherry for garnish

Pour the ingredients into a shaker with ice cubes. Shake well. Strain into a sour glass. Garnish with the cherry.

For a sour on the rocks, pour the ingredients into an old-fashioned glass. Stir well. Add ice cubes. Garnish with the cherry.

recipes

Abbey Cocktail

1 ¼ oz (37.5 mL) orange juice
1 ¼ oz (37.5 mL) gin
2 dashes orange bitters
maraschino cherry for garnish

Pour the ingredients into a shaker with ice cubes.
Shake well. Strain into a chilled cocktail glass.
Garnish with the cherry.

Adonis

1 oz (30 mL) dry sherry
½ oz (15 mL) sweet vermouth
½ oz (15 mL) dry vermouth
2 dashes orange bitters

Pour the ingredients into a mixing glass with ice cubes.
Stir well. Strain into a chilled cocktail glass.

Affinity

1 oz (30 mL) Scotch
½ oz (15 mL) dry vermouth
½ oz (15 mL) sweet vermouth
2 dashes orange bitters

Pour the ingredients into a mixing glass with ice
cubes. Stir well. Strain into a chilled cocktail glass.

Alexander

1 oz (30 mL) cream
1 oz (30 mL) crème de cacao (brown)
1 oz (30 mL) brandy
ground nutmeg for garnish

Pour the ingredients into a shaker with ice cubes. Shake well. Strain into a chilled cocktail glass. Garnish with a dusting of nutmeg.

This popular drink is also known as the Brandy Alexander.

Americano

1 oz (30 mL) Campari
1 oz (30 mL) sweet vermouth
club soda
lemon twist or orange slice for garnish

Fill an old-fashioned glass with ice cubes. Pour in the Campari and the vermouth. Add the club soda. Garnish with the lemon twist or orange slice.

The Americano provides a gentle introduction to the unusual taste of Campari. Switch to a highball glass and add more club soda for a definite thirst quencher.

Angel's Delight

1 ¼ oz (37.5 mL) cream
¾ oz (22.5 mL) triple sec
¾ oz (22.5 mL) gin
2–3 dashes grenadine

Pour the ingredients into a shaker with ice cubes. Shake well. Strain into a chilled cocktail glass.

B& B

1 oz (30 mL) Bénédictine
1 oz (30 mL) brandy

Pour the Bénédictine into a snifter. Use the back of a bar spoon to gently float the brandy on top.

Bacardi Cocktail

1 ¾ oz (52.5 mL) Bacardi light rum
¾ oz (22.5 mL) lemon or lime juice
¼ oz (7.5 mL) grenadine

Pour the ingredients into a shaker with ice cubes. Shake well. Strain into a chilled cocktail glass.

Beachcomber

1 ½ oz (45 mL) light rum
½ oz (15 mL) triple sec
½ oz (15 mL) lime juice
1 dash maraschino liqueur

Pour the ingredients into a shaker with ice cubes. Shake well. Strain into a chilled cocktail glass.

Bellini

2 oz (60 mL) peach juice or peach puree
4 oz (120 mL) Champagne

Pour the peach juice or peach puree into a Champagne flute. Slowly add the Champagne.

Between the Sheets or Maiden's Prayer

¾ oz (22.5 mL) brandy
¾ oz (22.5 mL) light rum
¾ oz (22.5 mL) triple sec
½ oz (15 mL) lemon juice
lemon twist for garnish

Pour the ingredients into a shaker with ice cubes.
Shake well. Strain into a chilled cocktail glass. Garnish
with the lemon twist.

Black Russian

1 ¾ oz (52.5 mL) vodka
¾ oz (22.5 mL) Kahlúa

Pour the ingredients into an old-fashioned glass
with ice cubes. Stir well.

Bloody Mary

3 oz (90 mL) tomato juice
1 ½ oz (45 mL) vodka
½ oz (15 mL) lemon juice
1 dash of Worcestershire sauce
celery salt
ground pepper
hot pepper sauce
celery stalk for garnish

Pour the liquid ingredients into a highball glass with ice
cubes. Mix well. Add the seasonings to taste. Garnish
with the celery stalk.

Blue Hawaiian

2 oz (60 mL) pineapple juice
¾ oz (22.5 mL) rum
¾ oz (22.5 mL) blue curaçao
¾ oz (22.5 mL) crème de coconut
maraschino cherry for garnish

Pour the ingredients into a mixing glass with ice cubes. Stir well. Strain into a collins glass filled with ice cubes. Garnish with the cherry.

Brandy Eggnog

1 ¼ oz (37.5 mL) milk
1 oz (30 mL) brandy
½ oz (15 mL) sugar syrup
1 egg yolk

Pour the ingredients into a shaker with ice cubes. Shake well. Strain into an old-fashioned glass.

Eggnog is also delicious made with bourbon, Irish whiskey, or rum.

Caipirinha

1 lime, quartered
1 tsp (5 mL) sugar syrup
2 oz (60 mL) cachaça

Place the lime wedges and the sugar syrup into an old-fashioned glass. Muddle well. Pour in the cachaça. Stir. Fill the glass with ice cubes. Stir again.

Campari Cocktail

1 oz (30 mL) Campari
¾ oz (22.5 mL) vodka
1 dash Angostura bitters
lemon twist for garnish

Pour the ingredients into a shaker with ice cubes. Shake well. Strain into a chilled cocktail glass. Garnish with the lemon twist.

Cape Codder

3 oz (90 mL) cranberry juice
1 ¼ oz (37.5 mL) vodka
lime wedge for garnish

Pour the ingredients into a highball glass with ice cubes. Stir. Squeeze the lime juice into the drink. Drop the lime wedge into the glass.

Champagne Cocktail

1 sugar cube
2–3 dashes Angostura bitters
Champagne
1 oz (30 mL) brandy
orange slice for garnish
maraschino cherry for garnish

Place the sugar cube in the bottom of a Champagne flute. Saturate the cube with the Angostura bitters. Pour the Champagne into the flute. Add the brandy. Garnish with the orange slice and the cherry.

Cosmopolitan

2 oz (60 mL) vodka
1 oz (30 mL) Cointreau
1 oz (30 mL) cranberry juice
½ oz (15 mL) lime juice
½ oz (15 mL) sugar syrup

Pour the ingredients into a shaker with ice cubes. Shake well. Strain into a chilled cocktail glass.

A sugar-rimmed glass flatters the taste and presentation of the Cosmopolitan. Add finely grated orange zest to the sugar for even more panache. A dash of orange bitters brings a superb variation in flavor to this drink.

Cuba Libre

½ lime
2 oz (60 mL) light rum
4 oz (120 mL) cola

Squeeze the juice of half a lime into a collins glass. Drop the lime into the glass. Add ice cubes. Pour the remaining ingredients into the glass. Stir well.

Daiquiri

1 ½ oz (45 mL) light rum
¾ oz (22.5 mL) lime juice
¼ oz (7.5 mL) sugar syrup

Pour the ingredients into a shaker with ice cubes. Shake well. Strain into a chilled cocktail glass.

Delilah or White Lady

1 ½ oz (45 mL) gin
¾ oz (22.5 mL) Cointreau
¾ oz (22.5 mL) lemon juice

Pour the ingredients into a shaker with ice cubes.
Shake well. Strain into a chilled cocktail glass.

Dubonnet Cocktail

1 oz (30 mL) Dubonnet
¾ oz (22.5 mL) gin
lemon twist for garnish

Pour the ingredients into a mixing glass with ice
cubes. Stir well. Strain into a chilled cocktail glass.
Garnish with the lemon twist.

French 75

¼ oz (7.5 mL) lemon juice
¼ oz (7.5 mL) gin
¼ oz (7.5 mL) Cointreau
5 oz (150 mL) Champagne

Pour the lemon juice, the gin, and the Cointreau
into a shaker with ice cubes. Shake well. Strain into
a chilled Champagne flute. Carefully add the
Champagne.

If you prefer, vodka can be substituted for gin.
This cocktail is called a French 76.

Fuzzy Navel

3 oz (90 mL) orange juice
1 oz (30 mL) vodka
1 oz (30 mL) peach liqueur

Pour the ingredients into an old-fashioned glass
with ice cubes. Stir well.

Gimlet

2 oz (60 mL) gin
1¾ oz (52.5 mL) lime juice

Pour the ingredients into a mixing glass with ice
cubes. Stir well. Strain into a chilled cocktail glass.

A variety of gimlets can be made. Simply substitute
another primary liquor for the gin. Rum, tequila,
and vodka are delicious alternatives.

Gin & It

¾ oz (22.5 mL) sweet vermouth
1½ oz (45 mL) gin
maraschino cherry for garnish

Pour the vermouth directly into a cocktail glass
without ice cubes. Add the gin. Garnish with
the cherry.

Gin & Tonic

2 oz (60 mL) gin
5 oz (150 mL) tonic water
lime wedge for garnish

Pour the ingredients into a highball glass with ice
cubes. Stir well. Garnish with the lime wedge.

Golden Cadillac

¾ oz (22.5 mL) cream
¾ oz (22.5 mL) crème de cacao, white
¾ oz (22.5 mL) Galliano

Pour the ingredients into a shaker with ice cubes.
Shake well. Strain into a chilled cocktail glass.

Golden Dawn

¾ oz (22.5 mL) gin
¾ oz (22.5 mL) apricot brandy
¾ oz (22.5 mL) calvados
¾ oz (22.5 mL) orange juice

Pour the ingredients into a shaker with ice cubes.
Shake well. Strain into a chilled cocktail glass.

Golden Dream

¾ oz (22.5 mL) cream
¾ oz (22.5 mL) orange juice
¾ oz (22.5 mL) Cointreau
¾ oz (22.5 mL) Galliano

Pour the ingredients into a shaker with ice cubes.
Shake well. Strain into a chilled cocktail glass.

Grasshopper

¾ oz (22.5 mL) cream
¾ oz (22.5 mL) crème de cacao, white
¾ oz (22.5 mL) crème de menthe, green

Pour the ingredients into a shaker with ice cubes.
Shake well. Strain into a chilled cocktail glass.

Greyhound or Salty Dog

2 oz (60 mL) vodka
4 oz (120 mL) grapefruit juice

Pour the ingredients into a collins glass with ice
cubes. Stir well.

—— **Grasshopper**

Harvey Wallbanger

¾ oz (22.5 mL) vodka
1½ oz (45 mL) orange juice
¼ oz (7.5 mL) Galliano
orange slice for garnish
maraschino cherry for garnish

Pour the vodka and the orange juice into a collins glass with ice cubes. Add the Galliano. Garnish with the orange slice and the cherry.

Horse's Neck

spiral lemon peel
2 oz (60 mL) brandy
8 oz (240 mL) ginger ale
2–3 dashes Angostura bitters (optional)

Place the spiral lemon peel into a collins glass. Secure one end of the peel over the lip of the glass. Add ice cubes to the glass. Pour the brandy and then the ginger ale. Add a dash of bitters if desired. Stir well.

Hot Buttered Rum

1 small slice of soft butter
1 tsp (5 mL) brown sugar
optional spices: ground cinnamon, ground nutmeg,
vanilla extract
2 oz (60 mL) dark rum
boiling water

Place the butter, the sugar, and the spices at the bottom of a hot drink mug. Mix well or muddle. Pour in the rum and the boiling water. Stir.

Hot Toddy

1½ oz (45 mL) blended whiskey
½ oz (15 mL) lemon juice
½ oz (15 mL) honey
¼ oz (7.5 mL) sugar syrup
hot water
lemon slice, whole cloves, and cinnamon stick for garnish

Pour the first four ingredients into a hot drink mug.
Stir well. Fill the mug with hot water. Stir again.
Garnish with the lemon slice spiked with the cloves,
and the cinnamon stick.

Hurricane

juice of half a lime
1 oz (30 mL) light rum
1 oz (30 mL) dark rum
¾ oz (22.5 mL) pineapple juice
¾ oz (22.5 mL) orange juice
¼ oz (7.5 mL) maracuja (passion fruit) syrup
lime wedge for garnish

Squeeze the juice from half a lime into a shaker
with ice cubes. Pour the remaining ingredients into
the shaker. Shake well. Strain into a highball glass
with ice cubes. Garnish with the lime wedge.

Imperial

1 oz (30 mL) dry vermouth
1 oz (30 mL) gin
1 tsp (5 mL) maraschino liqueur
lemon twist for garnish

Pour the ingredients into a mixing glass with ice
cubes. Stir well. Strain into a chilled cocktail glass.
Garnish with the lemon twist.

Irish Coffee

2 ½ oz (75 mL) strong, hot coffee
1 ½ oz (45 mL) Irish whiskey
1 tsp (5 mL) brown sugar
1 oz (30 mL) whipping cream

Pour the first three ingredients into a hot drink mug. Stir well. Float the cream on top.

Kamikaze

1 ½ oz (45 mL) vodka
1 oz (30 mL) lime juice
1 oz (30 mL) triple sec
lime wedge for garnish

Pour the ingredients into a shaker with ice cubes. Shake well. Strain into a chilled cocktail glass. Garnish with the lime wedge.

Kir

¼ oz (7.5 mL) crème de cassis
2 ¼ oz (67.5 mL) dry white wine

Pour the crème de cassis into a wine glass. Slowly add the dry white wine.

To make a Kir Royale, use a Champagne flute instead of a wine glass. Substitute Champagne for the dry white wine.

Lemon Drop

1 1/2 oz (45 mL) vodka
3/4 oz (22.5 mL) lemon juice
1 tsp (5 mL) sugar syrup
lemon twist for garnish

Pour the ingredients into a shaker with ice cubes. Shake well. Strain into a chilled cocktail glass. Garnish with the lemon twist.

Enhance the citrus flavor by adding 1/4 oz (7.5 mL) Cointreau and reducing the amount of sugar to 1/2 tsp (2.5 mL).

Long Island Iced Tea

1/2 oz (15 mL) triple sec
1/2 oz (15 mL) light rum
1/2 oz (15 mL) gin
1/2 oz (15 mL) vodka
1 oz (30 mL) lemon juice
cola

Pour the alcohol and the juice into a collins glass with ice. Stir well. Fill the remainder of the glass with the cola.

Madras

1 1/2 oz (45 mL) vodka
3 oz (90 mL) cranberry juice
1 oz (30 mL) orange juice

Pour the vodka and the cranberry juice into a highball glass with ice cubes. Stir well. Top with the orange juice.

Mai Tai

1 oz (30 mL) light rum
1 oz (30 mL) gold rum
½ oz (15 mL) lime juice
½ oz (15 mL) orange curaçao
½ oz (15 mL) orgeat syrup
1 oz (30 mL) dark rum
maraschino cherry for garnish

Pour all of the ingredients except the dark rum into a shaker with ice cubes. Shake well. Strain into an old-fashioned glass half filled with crushed ice. Top the drink with the dark rum. Garnish with the cherry.

Manhattan

1 ¼ oz (37.5 mL) Canadian whiskey
½ oz (15 mL) sweet vermouth
2–3 dashes Angostura bitters
maraschino cherry for garnish

Pour the ingredients into a mixing glass with ice cubes. Stir well. Strain into a chilled cocktail glass. Garnish with the cherry.

Margarita

1 ¼ oz (37.5 mL) tequila
¾ oz (22.5 mL) triple sec
½ oz (15 mL) lemon or lime juice
lime wedge for garnish
salt for garnish (optional)

Pour the ingredients into a shaker with ice cubes. Shake well. Strain into a chilled cocktail glass. Garnish with the lime wedge. Salt the rim of the glass before pouring the cocktail if desired.

Martinez

1 oz (30 mL) gin
¾ oz (22.5 mL) dry vermouth
¼ oz (7.5 mL) triple sec
1 dash orange bitters
lemon twist for garnish

Pour the ingredients into a mixing glass with ice
cubes. Stir well. Strain into a chilled cocktail glass.
Twist the lemon peel over the drink and drop it into
the glass.

Martini

1½ oz (45 mL) gin
½ tsp (2.5 mL) dry vermouth
1 green olive or lemon twist for garnish

Pour the ingredients into a mixing glass with ice
cubes. Stir well. Strain into a chilled martini glass.
Garnish with the olive or the lemon twist.

Personal preferences account for many variations in
creating this drink. Use equal parts of sweet and
dry vermouth for a perfect Martini, and garnish with
a lemon twist or a cherry. A Gibson is simply a dry
Martini garnished with a cocktail onion. Vodka
Martinis are a popular alternative; simply replace
the gin with vodka.

Melon Patch

1 oz (30 mL) melon liqueur
½ oz (15 mL) triple sec
½ oz (15 mL) vodka
4 oz (120 mL) club soda
orange slice for garnish

Pour the first three ingredients into a shaker with
ice cubes. Shake well. Strain into a highball glass
with ice cubes. Add the club soda. Garnish with the
orange slice.

Metropolitan

1 ½ oz (45 mL) brandy
1 oz (30 mL) sweet vermouth
½ tsp (2.5 mL) sugar syrup
2 dashes Angostura bitters

Pour the ingredients into a shaker with ice cubes. Shake well. Strain into a chilled cocktail glass.

Mint Julep

4–6 mint leaves
2 sugar cubes
4 oz (120 mL) bourbon
mint sprig for garnish

Place the ingredients into a cocktail shaker. Muddle well to dissolve the sugar and to release the oil and aroma of the mint. Add ice cubes to the shaker. Shake well. Strain into a collins glass with ice cubes. Garnish with the mint sprig.

Mojito

2 tsp (10 mL) sugar
6–8 mint leaves
club soda
1 lime, halved
2 oz (60 mL) light rum
mint sprig for garnish

Place the sugar, the mint leaves, and a little club soda into a highball glass. Muddle well to dissolve the sugar and to release the mint flavor. Squeeze the juice from both halves of the lime into the glass. Drop one half of the lime into the glass. Add the rum. Stir. Fill the glass with ice cubes. Add the rest of the club soda. Garnish with the mint sprig.

Monkey Gland

2 oz (60 mL) gin
1 oz (30 mL) orange juice
¼ oz (7.5 mL) grenadine
1 dash Pernod
orange slice for garnish

Pour the ingredients into a shaker with ice cubes. Shake well. Strain into a chilled cocktail glass. Garnish with the orange slice.

Negroni

¾ oz (22.5 mL) sweet vermouth
¾ oz (22.5 mL) Campari
¾ oz (22.5 mL) gin
orange slice for garnish

Pour the ingredients into an old-fashioned glass with ice cubes. Stir well. Garnish with the orange slice.

New Orleans Fizz or Ramos Fizz

1 ½ oz (45 mL) gin
½ oz (15 mL) lime juice
½ oz (15 mL) lemon juice
½ oz (15 mL) powdered sugar
¼ oz (7.5 mL) cream
1 egg white
3–4 dashes fleurs d'orange (orange flower water)
¼ oz (7.5 mL) club soda

Place all of the ingredients into a shaker with ice cubes. Shake vigorously. Strain into a chilled wine glass.

Old-Fashioned

1 sugar cube
2–3 dashes Angostura bitters
2 orange slices
2 oz (60 mL) bourbon
$\frac{1}{2}$ oz (15 mL) club soda
maraschino cherry for garnish

Place the sugar cube at the bottom of an old-fashioned glass, and saturate the cube with the bitters. Add one orange slice. Muddle these ingredients. Fill the glass with ice cubes. Add the bourbon and the club soda. Stir well. Garnish with the second orange slice and the cherry.

Park Avenue

1 $\frac{1}{2}$ oz (45 mL) gin
$\frac{1}{4}$ oz (7.5 mL) dry vermouth
$\frac{1}{4}$ oz (7.5 mL) sweet vermouth
$\frac{1}{4}$ oz (7.5 mL) unsweetened pineapple juice

Pour the ingredients into a mixing glass with ice cubes. Stir well. Strain into a chilled cocktail glass.

Pimm's

2 oz (60 mL) Pimm's No. 1
3 oz (90 mL) lemon-lime soda
lemon twist for garnish
cucumber peel or slice for garnish

Pour the Pimm's into a collins glass with ice cubes. Add the lemon-lime soda. Garnish with the lemon twist and the cucumber peel or slice.

Make a Pimm's Rangoon by substituting ginger ale for lemon-lime soda, or try a Pimm's Royal by using Champagne.

Piña Colada

2 ¹/₂ oz (75 mL) pineapple juice
1 ¹/₂ oz (45 mL) light rum
1 oz (30 mL) coconut cream
pineapple wedge for garnish

Pour the ingredients into a mixing glass with
crushed ice. Stir well. Pour into a chilled cocktail
glass. Garnish with the pineapple wedge.

Pink Gin or Gin & Bitters

1 ¹/₂ oz (45 mL) gin
3–4 dashes Angostura bitters

Pour the ingredients into a shaker with ice cubes.
Shake well. Strain into a chilled cocktail glass.

Pink Lady

1 ¹/₂ oz (45 mL) gin
¹/₄ oz (7.5 mL) lemon juice
1–2 dashes grenadine
1 egg white
maraschino cherry for garnish

Pour the ingredients into a shaker with ice cubes.
Shake well. Strain into a chilled cocktail glass.
Garnish with the cherry.

Planter's Punch

1 1/2 oz (45 mL) dark rum
3/4 oz (22.5 mL) lemon juice
1/4 oz (7.5 mL) grenadine
club soda
maraschino cherry for garnish
lemon slice for garnish

Pour all of the ingredients, except the club soda, into a shaker with ice cubes. Shake well. Strain into a highball glass with ice cubes. Fill the glass with the club soda. Garnish with the lemon slice and the cherry.

Red Snapper

1 oz (30 mL) light rum
1 oz (30 mL) cream
3/4 oz (22.5 mL) Galliano
1 dash grenadine

Pour the ingredients into a shaker with ice cubes. Shake well. Strain into a chilled cocktail glass.

Rob Roy

1 1/2 oz (45 mL) Scotch
1 oz (30 mL) sweet vermouth
1 dash Angostura bitters
maraschino cherry for garnish

Pour the ingredients into a mixing glass with ice cubes. Stir well. Strain into a chilled cocktail glass. Garnish with the cherry.

This drink can be made perfect by splitting the amount of vermouth between sweet and dry.

Rusty Nail

1 1/2 oz (45 mL) Scotch
3/4 oz (22.5 mL) Drambuie
lemon twist for garnish

Pour the ingredients into an old-fashioned glass with ice cubes. Stir well. Garnish with the lemon twist.

Sazerac

1 sugar cube
1 dash Peychaud bitters
2 oz (60 mL) rye whiskey
1/2 tsp (2.5 mL) Pernod
water or club soda

Place the sugar cube at the bottom of an old-fashioned glass. Saturate the cube with a dash of bitters. Muddle. Add the whiskey and the Pernod. Mix well. Fill the glass with the water or club soda. This drink is always served neat.

Scorpion

juice of half a lime
1 1/2 oz (45 mL) orange juice
3/4 oz (22.5 mL) brandy
3/4 oz (22.5 mL) light rum
3/4 oz (22.5 mL) dark rum
1/4 oz (7.5 mL) triple sec
lime wedge for garnish

Squeeze the lime juice into a shaker with ice cubes. Add all of the other ingredients. Shake well. Strain into a highball glass with ice cubes. Garnish with the lime wedge.

Screwdriver

2 oz (60 mL) vodka
5 oz (150 mL) orange juice

Pour the ingredients into a collins glass with ice cubes. Stir well.

Sea Breeze

1 ¾ oz (52.5 mL) vodka
3 oz (90 mL) cranberry juice
1 oz (30 mL) grapefruit juice
grapefruit slice for garnish

Pour the vodka and the cranberry juice into a high ball glass with ice cubes. Stir well. Top the drink with the grapefruit juice. Garnish with the grapefruit slice.

Shirley Temple, nonalcoholic

3 oz (90 mL) lemon-lime soda
3 oz (90 mL) ginger ale
1 dash grenadine
maraschino cherry for garnish

Pour the lemon-lime soda and the ginger ale into a collins glass with ice cubes. Add a dash of grenadine. Stir. Garnish with the cherry.

Sidecar

1 ½ oz (45 mL) Cognac
¾ oz (22.5 mL) Cointreau
¼ oz (7.5 mL) lemon juice

Pour the ingredients into a shaker with ice cubes. Shake well. Strain into a chilled cocktail glass.

Singapore Sling

1 1/2 oz (45 mL) gin
1 oz (30 mL) lemon juice
1/4 oz (7.5 mL) sugar syrup
1 1/2 tsp (7.5 mL) powdered sugar
2 oz (60 mL) club soda
1/2 oz (15 mL) cherry brandy
lemon slice for garnish
maraschino cherry for garnish

Pour the first four ingredients into a shaker with ice cubes. Shake well. Strain into a highball glass with ice cubes. Pour in the club soda. Float the cherry brandy on top. Garnish with the lemon slice and the cherry.

Stinger

1 3/4 oz (52.5 mL) brandy
3/4 oz (22.5 mL) crème de menthe, white

Pour the ingredients into an old-fashioned glass with crushed ice. Stir well. This drink can also be shaken over ice cubes and strained into a chilled cocktail glass.

Tequila Sunrise

4 oz (120 mL) orange juice
2 oz (60 mL) tequila
1/2 oz (15 mL) grenadine
orange slice for garnish
maraschino cherry for garnish

Pour the tequila and the orange juice into a highball glass with ice cubes. Stir. Carefully top the drink with the grenadine. Garnish with the orange slice and the cherry.

Tequila Sunrise

Tom Collins

1¹/₂ oz (45 mL) gin
1 oz (30 mL) lemon juice
¹/₂ oz (15 mL) sugar syrup
2 oz (60 mL) club soda
maraschino cherry for garnish
lemon slice for garnish

Pour the gin, the lemon juice, and the sugar syrup into a collins glass with ice cubes. Stir thoroughly. Add the club soda. Garnish with the cherry and the lemon slice.

Ward Eight

1³/₄ oz (52.5 mL) bourbon
¹/₂ oz (15 mL) lemon juice
¹/₂ oz (15 mL) orange juice
1 tsp (5 mL) grenadine
maraschino cherry for garnish

Pour the ingredients into a shaker with ice cubes. Shake well. Strain into a chilled cocktail glass. Garnish with the cherry.

Whiskey Sour

1¹/₂ oz (45 mL) bourbon
1¹/₂ oz (45 mL) lemon juice
³/₄ oz (22.5 mL) sugar syrup
maraschino cherry for garnish

Pour the ingredients into a shaker with ice cubes. Shake well. Strain into a chilled sour glass. Garnish with the cherry.

Sours can also be made with Scotch or other whiskeys.

White Russian

1 1/2 oz (45 mL) vodka
3/4 oz (22.5 mL) Kahlúa
3/4 oz (22.5 mL) cream

Pour the vodka and Kahlúa into an old-fashioned glass with ice cubes. Stir. Gently top the drink with the cream.

Yellow Bird

juice of half a lime
1 1/4 oz. (37.5 mL) orange juice
1 oz (30 mL) light rum
1 oz (30 mL) dark rum
1/4 oz (7.5 mL) Galliano
maraschino cherry for garnish

Squeeze the lime juice into a shaker with ice. Add all of the remaining ingredients. Shake well. Strain into a collins glass with crushed ice. Garnish with the cherry.

Zombie

1 1/4 oz (37.5 mL) lemon juice
1 oz (30 mL) dark rum
3/4 oz (22.5 mL) orange juice
1/2 oz (15 mL) cherry brandy
1/2 oz (15 mL) light rum
1/2 oz (15 mL) high-proof dark rum
2 dashes grenadine

Pour the ingredients into a shaker with ice cubes. Shake well. Strain into a highball glass with crushed ice.

acknowledgments

_M_any thanks to those who abundantly gave of their time, talent, and assets to create this book. Special recognition goes to: Terri Adams, of Hip Replacements, and Sandra Stambaugh, both fantastic collectors of vintage cocktail accoutrements; Complements to the Chef, in Asheville, North Carolina, an incredible (and incredibly generous) cooking and entertaining emporium; Pier 1 Imports; and Charlton Fyne, whose taste, intelligence, and imagination will always be an inspiration.

Drink Guide

Aperitifs

Adonis
Affinity
Americano
Campari Cocktail
Dubonnet Cocktail
Gibson
Gimlet
Gin & Bitters
Gin & It
Gin & Tonic
Imperial
Kir
Manhattan
Martinez
Martini
Negroni
Park Avenue
Pimm's
Pink Gin
Rob Roy

Brandy Drinks

Alexander
B & B
Between the Sheets
Brandy Eggnog

Champagne Cocktail
Golden Dawn
Horse's Neck
Maiden's Prayer
Metropolitan
Scorpion
Sidecar
Singapore Sling
Stinger
Zombie

Brunch Drinks

Bellini
Bloody Mary
Cape Codder
Gin & Tonic
Greyhound
Madras
Melon Patch
Salty Dog
Sea Breeze
Screwdriver

Campari Drinks

Americano
Campari Cocktail
Negroni

Cachaça Drink

Caipirinha

Champagne Cocktails

Bellini
Champagne Cocktail
French 75
French 76
Kir Royale
Pimm's Royal

Cream Drinks

Alexander
Angel's Delight
Brandy Eggnog
Golden Cadillac
Golden Dream
Grasshopper
Irish Coffee
New Orleans Fizz
Ramos Fizz
Red Snapper
White Russian

Digestifs

Alexander
Angel's Delight
B & B
Black Russian
Golden Cadillac
Golden Dream
Grasshopper
Red Snapper
Rusty Nail
White Russian

Drinks Suitable for the Blender

Brandy Eggnog
Daiquiri
Grasshopper
Margarita
Piña Colada
White Russian

Gin Drinks

Abbey Cocktail
Angel's Delight
Delilah
Dubonnet Cocktail
French 75
Gibson
Gimlet
Gin & Bitters
Gin & It
Gin & Tonic
Golden Dawn
Imperial
Long Island Iced Tea
Martinez
Martini
Monkey Gland
Negroni

New Orleans Fizz
Park Avenue
Pink Gin
Pink Lady
Ramos Fizz
Singapore Sling
Tom Collins
White Lady

Hot Drinks

Hot Buttered Rum
Hot Toddy
Irish Coffee

Identical Drinks

Between the Sheets
    and Maiden's Prayer
Delilah and White Lady
Greyhound and Salty Dog
New Orleans Fizz and
    Ramos Fizz
Pink Gin and Gin & Bitters

Nonalcoholic Drinks

Shirley Temple

Pimm's Drinks

Pimm's
Pimm's Rangoon
Pimm's Royal

Pitcher Drinks

Bloody Mary
Daiquiri
Fuzzy Navel
Hurricane
Kamikaze
Margarita
Piña Colada

Rum Drinks

Bacardi Cocktail
Beachcomber
Between the Sheets
Blue Hawaiian
Cuba Libre
Daiquiri
Hot Buttered Rum
Hurricane
Long Island Iced Tea
Mai Tai
Maiden's Prayer
Mojito
Piña Colada
Planter's Punch
Red Snapper
Scorpion
Yellow Bird
Zombie

Sherry Drink

Adonis

Tequila Drinks

Margarita
Tequila Sunrise

Vermouth Drinks

Adonis
Affinity
Americano
Gin & It
Imperial
Manhattan
Martinez
Martini
Metropolitan
Negroni
Park Avenue
Rob Roy

Vodka Drinks

Black Russian
Bloody Mary
Campari Cocktail
Cape Codder
Cosmopolitan
Fuzzy Navel

Greyhound
Harvey Wallbanger
Kamikaze
Lemon Drop
Long Island Iced Tea
Madras
Melon Patch
Salty Dog
Sea Breeze
Screwdriver
White Russian

Wine Cocktail

Kir

Whiskey Drinks, Canadian or Blended

Hot Toddy
Manhattan

Whiskey Drinks, Bourbon

Mint Julep
Old-Fashioned
Ward Eight
Whiskey Sour

Whiskey Drinks, Irish

Irish Coffee

Whiskey Drinks, Rye

Sazerac

Whiskey Drinks, Scotch

Affinity
Rob Roy
Rusty Nail

Drink Index

General Index